T0105668

HOW TO RAISE A CHILD

BY JULIA BULLARD

Order this book online at www.trafford.com
or email orders@trafford.com

Most Trafford titles are also available at major online book retailers.

Printed in the United States of America.

ISBN: 978-1-4269-6582-1 (sc)
ISBN: 978-1-4269-6583-8 (e)

Trafford rev. 05/17/2011

 www.trafford.com

North America & international
toll-free: 1 888 232 4444 (USA & Canada)
phone: 250 383 6864 ✦ fax: 812 355 4082

INTRODUCTION

I have realized that I survived while raising my son and now that he is a "teen" I'd like to share my parental knowledge on how to raise your child before he or she becomes a teen.

My purpose for writing this book is that I want to be able to share my parental knowledge with all parents who feel they don't know where to start when they begin parenting. By being parents you create your own manual on how to raise your own child and this is how you start.

CHAPTER 1
BEGINNING OF LIFE

To form a new life, all it takes is for one male's sperm and one female's egg to meet. When the egg and the sperm meet in the female's embryo, they bond together. Out of that, a new human being will be formed. Now that is where the woman has realized that she has formed a human being. So now it is time to learn and know how to take care of this new human being that is being formed inside her embryo for nine months.

When a baby is born, it is considered that from the embryo of the woman, whom the baby comes out, she is considered the biological mother. It is going to be her responsibility to nurture and raise that baby which has formed in her embryo. That mother is going to need to raise, discipline and teach that child what it is going to need to know to be able to survive and live a happy life. A woman whom is the mother of the newborn has control over how she wants her newborn to be raised while growing up. If the woman never heard her newborn cry while inside her embryo, than why allow it now? We know that when a baby cries, it is their only way of saying that it wants something.

That's fine. Just nurture the baby when it is needed than continue your day. As the mother you need to make an everyday daily schedule. Most important you have to stick with that daily schedule and not just once in awhile. The baby needs to realize how it is going to be treated for what reasons and at what time. Believe me, babies already know more than you think they do. You are going to have to get use to your baby when it cries. It is good for them to cry so that they can get it all out until they realize that crying is not working. Before you know it, your baby has stopped crying and knows that you will not give it any attention when it is crying. That will be your biggest relief. It takes awhile to learn how to do something that is being taught. We don't just go to a corner and pout just......

What is good and what is bad, what we brought them into this world for, who is mom and who is dad, and how to respect and listen to mom and dad and why they need to be raised the way mom and dad are raising them. But we don't just tell our baby all this just once. Oh No! You need to repeat and remind your baby everyday of your baby's life. Before you know it you will see that your baby will know more than what you thought your baby was going to know by a certain age. Now both parents need to compromise on a lot of things before ever mentioning it to their baby. It wouldn't be fair for your baby to listen to mom and dad and they are not on the same subject. Your baby does not need to grow up listening to mom and dad and neither is making sense. Your baby didn't ask you to bring it into this world, and if this is the kind of life you are going to teach it then it wouldn't be fair, now would it? As happy and fun as it was building your baby than that is how fun you should continue by raising your baby the correct and best way you know how. Most of all, be patient and I do promise you, that you and your baby will go a long way living a great life together. Of course, if you are an only parent, you will think it is going to be tough to raise a baby. "No' nothing is tough in life, if we ourselves believe that we can do it no matter what. Learn to have trust in yourself. Start believing in yourself, nobody else will believe in you unless you do yourself. After that, things will get easier everyday for both you and your baby. You always need to remember to give your baby something new everyday to know or do plus you need to grow with your baby. Don't stay behind and keep treating your baby like a newborn when it already outgrew all that. You have to grow with your baby or else your baby will leave you behind and move on by itself. That is sad when that happens. But you think about it and figure out whose fault would it be? Yes, yours! You need to always remember that your baby is growing every hour of the day. Your baby will be alive more in getting older than being a baby. Grow and treat your baby by the age it is and not by the age you enjoy most of them. That way you will both live a fantastic happy life.

LIFE PATH

In order to maintain your child on the right path of life, as parents you need to walk that *life path* with your child, and teach, train, discipline, and educate your child while walking that *life path* together. It might sound or feel like it is a lifetime path to walk, maybe it is, but it will be worth it. Once you get to the part of the *life path* where you begin to realize just how much your child has picked up from you, and who was there with you helping you with your child, you will then realize it was worth every step on the way. Parents need to spend more quality time with their child. By doing that, you might not realize it, but it teaches a lot to your child about what you want your child to learn. Giving your child money, presents, trips and any of the other items you give your child is not what your child has been hoping to get from you! All you child wishes to get from you is "Time." Hard to believe it but that is it! It seems the easier it is, the less you want to give. But because everything you want to give your child costs money and since you have worked for it, you would like to share it with your child, the child you love very much. In real life when we have a lot to give and share, we give it and share it with that one person whom we come out loving for the rest of our lives. That is usually the only way we know how to show someone we love him or her. If you think about it, a lot of what you have should not always be given to the one you love because they can become by nature, greedy. You run the risk losing everything just for wanting to share it. Sorry, but it is the same with a child, if you do or give to much to your child, your child will become a greedy, snooty little brat. You don't realize it but that is exactly what you don't want your child to become in life. It is much simpler to just walk the *life path* with your child and really teach your child how to see life. To see what is the correct way to live the great life awarded to him or her in this big world of ours that has been waiting for your child. There is nothing wrong with giving things to your child, but you should only give a thing to your child as a reward, when your child has really deserved it. Oh, and don't give too much or exaggerate on it. Think of when you eat, when you stuff yourself you gain those pounds you were hoping not too gain. Whose fault is it? Yes, yours! Just don't stuff yourself. It is the same as giving things to your child. Don't give to much and don't think that it has to cost a lot either. Your child will always appreciate what you give him or her no matter where you bought it or how much you spent on it. Parents don't realize it but they start teaching their child just the things they hope their child does not do in the future. Parents need to really be sure if parenting is what they want to do for the next 18 years or more before even having sex with their partners. You know if you put the time it took to make your child than you are going to need to put that much time plus for your child when he/she is born. It is just not fair for your child if you don't. your child did not ask to come into this world, your partner and you created him or her and now you and your partner need to teach your child how to grow and what it takes to be the best. This is why you and your partner really need to think straight before jumping into that bed and regretting it afterwards. Parenting is a great career but if you really don't enjoy being with children, then you won't enjoy parenting either. Of course, you can start learning parenting if you badly want children. Anything is possible to learn it just depends on how much time you are willing to spend to learn that certain career. Remember, most of us don't learn everything we need to know on parenting, most of it is an intuition that is always been inside of you just waiting for you to decide to use it so it will come out. Parenting is easy; it just depends on how you see it and how you use it. It becomes fun and in time you will want to know more and even share it with your good friends. Never give up on your child. Always be proud of what your child has accomplished in life no matter what, even if you think there should have been more. All that your child wants from you as a parent is your love and to be proud at times. That's all your child wants and needs from you. Is that considered too much for you as a parent to give?

CHAPTER 2
BABY'S POWER

Your own baby can easily take control over you and your spouse. I know right now you do not believe this. Well its very true. You see soon your baby is born you don't know exactly how to show your baby that you love it very much no matter what. So you think that by giving your baby everything your baby wants that's going to really show your baby you really love it. "Nope" if you do you're already starting to raise it wrong. Soon your baby is born it needs to know whose mom and whose dad. Well you started by not always giving your baby too much attention when it really isn't necessary. You think about your times when your sweetheart gave you something and it dint solve your problem, instead you were hoping your sweetheart would of just given you a hug or at least talk to you about your situation, wouldn't you say that it would of solve your problem possibly? Babies are the same way, you don't think they understand you when you're talking to them but believe me they do. Don't let your baby fool you. Don't let your baby lead or else life is going to be a pain while raising your baby. You need to set rules to your baby and make sure you stick with them and your baby does too. Babies don't understand everything clearly but they do understand most of it, just watch them when you finished talking to them and you'll see the different changes your child makes once your child finished listening to you. Your baby will get an understanding message if you don't attend it every time it cries or loses its temper. This is where you as the parent should have a good control on it. Learn early to be "very" patient with your baby or else nothing will work out the way you're expecting it to. If you know your baby is healthy, full and clean than there's nothing to worry about, just go check on your baby, if the diaper is not wet, theirs no itching and everything looks fine than leave your baby alone and let it cry or lose its temper until it calms down. Now, once its calm down than that's when you play with your baby. That's teaching your child that if he/she doesn't cry nor lose its temper for no good reasons than sure you'll pick him/her up and you'll play. After a while your baby will recognize that you won't pick him/her up if he/she cries or lose temper. Of course this'll take a while for your baby to know the difference, but once your baby gets it that's it. You tell me why did it take so long for your beautiful baby to be born? That's right because that's how long it always takes when you want something as perfect as your baby to be build and born. You were patient, weren't you? But than of course you didn't have any choice if you wanted a healthy child. Right? This is exactly what you'll always need to remember about training your baby and why it takes so long for your baby to understand you. Most of all you need to remember the rules you gave your baby and how it is you want your baby to follow it. If your boss keeps changing the rules they gave you about work, how would you feel? That's right, you'll feel like screaming at your boss just to get it out of you, since you weren't told why certain rules got changed. A time only when your baby would need

7

extra attention from you or your spouse is when your baby is born with some kind of sickness. That's very understanding. But if your baby just wants to be carried around most of the day just because your baby likes being held, well that is a very "wrong" reason. You'll soon realize that you have a life to live and responsibilities to take care of and that carrying your own baby just because your baby wants to be carried like that all day, that is your biggest mistake you've made with your baby. You can correct it right now, believe me anything is possible and true so try it. You'll realize that after carrying your baby for so long and than this idea about not carrying it is so much nor giving it everything it wants does work with you, you'll never regret it plus it would be a big relief to you. A little bit of free time to a parent is better than no time at all.

CHAPTER 3
DISCIPLINE

To discipline your child means to teach your child how to follow rules training your child's mind and body how it should be while your child is growing. The best age you should start disciplining your child is usually when you've realized that your child has begun to understand you, this usually doesn't matter what age your child is in. nothing in life is never too early to begin with your own child. Yes it can start at a very young age, like when your child turns into months old and not years old. You should know that the younger you start disciplining your child the better it'll be for both of you. You'll be able to teach your child more and more. And your child will be ready for life at an early age which will be "great" you'll never regret doing it this way. There's a lot to know and remember when disciplining your child. You need to know exactly what is the subject you want to start on disciplining your child and you need to remember it plus you need to remember what you taught your child on that certain subject and in what order you've taught your child its not fair that your child gets either in trouble or punished when it might have been your fault as the adult not to remember what you've been teaching your child. No matter what subject you select to discipline your child with you'll always need to repeat it a lot to your child until you've realize that your child has memorized it and knows what it means to do when mom and dad say it. Now the biggest problems parents as couples have, are that both parents are not willing to go along with what one of the parent says. That when it becomes a very big problem in the parents life and especially in their child's life too. Both want the best for their child but are not willing to cooperate together. That's where parents are just going to either let one parent do the disciplines or both parents are going to have to work together at it. It's not fair to the child, because the child will get nothing out of the parents if they're just going to argue when it comes to disciplining their own child. Its great that the child is loved very much by both parents, but its hard if they both can't train their child about what real life is out there in this big world we've all are living in. parents need to remember that their child is born with a very clear clean mind. They as parents are the ones whom are going to fill up their child's mind with what they think is right and wrong for their child. Parents need to be careful on that part when disciplining their child, once a parent said something, their child picks it up real fast. Parents can't erase certain words they've said to their child because its their child's mind already. Got to watch and hear what you're going to say in front of your child. If parents aren't careful about what they teach their child, they'll regret it, but it'll be too late so its just better to be careful about what we're planning to say when we're in front of the child. These are certain words needed to discipline your own child: thank you, hi, hello, good bye, excuse me, would you please hand me…, your welcome, can you please…, could you please…, please hand me…, please give me…, can I please…, may I please…, can I please have a…, can I please have one…, will you please…

DISCIPLINE

To discipline your child means to teach your child how to follow rules, training your child's mind and body. How it should be while your child is growing. The best age you should start disciplining your child is usually when you realized that your child had began to understand you, this usually doesn't matter what age your child is in. Nothing in life is never too early to begin with your own child. Yes it could start at a very young age, like when your child turns into months old and not years old. You should know that the younger you start disciplining your child the better it'll be for both of you. You'll be able to teach your child more and more. And your child will be ready for life at an early age which will be "great" you'll never regret doing it this way. There's a lot to know and remember when disciplining your child and you need to remember it plus you need to remember what you tought your child on that certain subject and in what order you've . . . taught your child. It's not your fault that your child gets either in trouble or punished when it might have been your fault as the adult not to remember what you've been teaching your child, no matter what subject you select to discipline your child with you'll always need to repeat it a lot to your child until you've realized that your child has memorized it and knows what it means to do when mom or dad says it. Now the biggest problems parents as couples have are that both parents are not willing to go along with what one of the parents says.

That's when it becomes a very big problem in the parents' life and especially in their child's life too. Both wants the best for their child but are not willing to cooperate together. Thats where parents are just going to either let one parent do the disciplines or both parents are going to have to work together at it. It's not fair to the child, because the child will get nothing out of the parents if their just going to argue with when it comes to disciplining their own child. it's great that a child is loved very much by both parents, but its hard if no that both can't train their child about what real life is out there in this big world we're all are living in. Parents need to remember that their child is born with a very clear clean mind. They as parents are the ones whom are going to fill up their child's mind with what they think what's right and wrong for their child. Parents need to be careful on that part when disciplining their child. Once a parent said something their child picks it up real fast. Parents can't erase certain words they've said to their child because it's inside their child's mind already.gotta watch and hear what you're going to say in front of your child. If parents aren't careful about what they teach their child. They'll regret it, but it'll be too late so it's just better to be careful about what we're planning to say when you're in front of the child. These are certain words needed to discipline to your own child: thank you, hi.hello, bye, excuse me, would you please hand me…... please hand me…,your welcome, can you please… ,could you please…,please hand me…,please give me… can I please…,may I please …,can I please have a …can I please have a …, can I please have one, will you please… all these plus i'm sure you'll have more to add on the list, should be the first vocabulary you start your child with, of course you'd want your child to first start with mom and dad. Being an only parent would be easier that way you don't have to talk it over with anyone, if you know its right you'll do it, of course you won't no, of you for a fact that it's wrong. These expressions I've written to start your child with on his/ her first words of discipline, it can be used in any languages all over the world as their first vocabulary too. From when our child is small what we want most from them is respect whether it's to us the parents or to people when their with they're parents when they aren't around.

Childs daily discipline

These are some of the disciplines that should be reminded daily to your child:

.Respect parents do as parents say

Respect adults

.Do not answer back

.Don't use bad words

.Always thank the person for anything they give or do for you

.never accept anything from any strangers

.Never Speak to strangers

.Behave you're self whether it's at home or in the public

.Excuse yourself

Never interrupt people while they're talking, excuse yourself

Use your table manners: (don't chew with your mouth open, keep elbows of the table, sit-up straight, hold silverware correctly, don't talk while chewing, excuse yourself before leaving, don't gargle the liquid, don't burp, don't play with food etc.)

Be polite to people you meet, shake hands, smile, give your name and ask for theirs.

Do not disturb nor interrupt anyone while on the phone

Never give order to an adult

Always say please when needed

Do not touch anything with out permission from the owner

ETC….

I'm sure you have a little more to add. But if you would see that these are done daily before you realize your child and you will be happy.

CHAPTER 4

SHOWING LOVE TO YOUR CHILD

Gosh! The finest and best way you can show your child that you love your child is just by telling your child "I love you" but really meaning it when you say it to your child. That's it, easy isn't it? But you know there are parents that don't really know this and others that don't believe it why? Because they must have been raised differently. Other way, parents believe to tell their child they love 'em, would be giving the child anything that child wants, doing anything for their child, (kind of like being the child's slave) sorry to say but boy are those very wrong ways to use to tell your child you love 'em .because that's raising your child the wrong way for sure. Think of this: was your child born with stuff or was your child just born and felt happy when your child realized who the parents were? So then why can't parents grasp that and continue it while raising their child? As parents you don't need to be stucked with your child nor be giving the child hugs, kisses, lovie duyi cost every minete, my gosh don't you think about yourself too, you need time for yourself everyday

. Well, what you don't want done to you than don't teach it nor do it to your child so many times in a day. NA child imitates everything that's done to him/her (especially by mom or dad) plus if that's the thing you do to your child always than that's the only thing your child is going to do. Why do parents begin talking to their child as grown –ups after their teen years, what's the different, you waited this long to show your child that your child need to know how to take care of his/her responsibility so its now time to grow-up and for your child to get his/her act together. Boy is that wrong! Who's to blame if the child doesn't know anything else but baby stuff. That's right the parents, yes, there is a way to teach it to your child, what's wrong with that? Teach your baby to put its own toys away, fix the bed, not to interrupt, when its time to play, when your baby needs to use the toilet, when you want time alone etc…I'm sure you'd have more. Train to your child. If a dog is never too old to do new tricks than your child is not too young to learn responsibilities, the minute your youngster, cab crawl, walks and talks and understands, it's time to start training. You don't realize this but your child would want to learn so much besides coochy coos so that he/she can feel so good, happy and proud of themselves, of course they couldn't tell you this, but I believe if your child could, your child would tell you this. There's nothing wrong wanting to show and tell your child you love 'em so much, just don't go over board you'll see how happy you both could be. "Love" has the cheapest price on it, so why not use it the right way. The best source to a child is that if you really love your child than you as parents will give it all you got from your mind and see that your child goes down the right path. Your child will always need you as parents. By giving your child that love you really have for your child, your child will always be happy and so sure inside his/her heart and mind that your child will always know he/she can count on his/her parents no matter what it's about, if he/she has a problem or is in trouble. You don't believe this but your child builds his own world around 'em depending how you raised 'em. Love from you will always be the guaranteed for sure inside 'em.

SHOWING YOUR LOVE WITH YOUR CHILD

If you as parents have a good pair of ears to listen with and heart to love back at your child, than you'll need to know how to share your love with your child. You know your child isn't asking for much from you, of course they always want your love and attention at a time when you just can't give it to them. Well that's when you as the parents explain to your child that love and attention can not always be given to them at exactly when they expect it. Plus love and attention for some reason it's the hardest 2 things for parents to give to their child. Mostly because a parent doesn't make quality time for it or the parent just doesn't care for the love and attention their child needs. As parents we can't blame our child for coming into this world, the child never asked to come, as parents you both had sex and constructed your child and as the mother you ate the right food to keep your child healthy and strong while growing in your stomach. Now you both need to share those 2 special important parts of your life with your child love and your 2 good ears to listen to your child. As parents you're going to need to know what kind of love and how much to share with your child. You don't need to share all your energy with your child every day, you need to realize that there's nothing wrong with that. You'll be needing your own energy all day too for your own home responsibilities "don't forget that" plus the world does not revolve around you unless you move and take care of your responsibilities.

CHAPTER 5
DOING OUR BEST

Of course as parents you would always want the best for your child. Well, the best you can give your child is the best you know how. This means trying your hardest in teaching your child how to do certain things in life while growing up For Example: you should've been looking at your child into it's eyes every time you spoke to 'em and made sure your child was looking at you too, that way you knew your child was listening, concentrating and paying attention to what you were telling 'em. That trains the child to always look at a person into the face when their talking to them. GREET: shake hands always when you're being introduce and say your name

Every morning say "good morning"
Every night say "good night"

Always say "thank you" for everything that is given or handed to you. Wave when you're being waved. Always say "excuse me" when you want to leave and there's other people around. Apologize if it's your fault. Train your child how to use the toilet the correct way plus cleaning after themselves always when finished. Especially when they visit people. How to get anywhere your child goes, for this you need "patience" because this takes a lot of discipline before your child gets the hang of it with no problem and doing it automatically what you trained the child to do and not to do. No your child is not a robot but if you don't control your child with heavy discipline. The child then will control you. You should teach your child to care for thing whether it belongs to 'em or not. Of course as parents you should never find it funny when you're training your child because your child won't take it serious. If you have to laugh so much than take a break. When parents train they need to be serious and try to explain the subject to the child the easiest way that child would understand about what's going on. Your child will soon outgrow this baby talk of those while being a kid. Keep in mind that your child will be an adult longer that it will as a child. It's hard, but it's ready to care for itself without you while growing –up. Then let your child do it on its own and you do your own things, just move-on. Your child will come to you when it needs you so don't worry. You'll always be that best teacher your child ever had. If you don't feel comfortable this way then talk to someone about how you feel, since it's not a satisfaction to you: a counselor, family doctor, good friend or maybe just yourself in your mirror to make sure you know you've done everything with in your power. You know anyone can really do this job if they really set themselves to it with out any college degree. All it takes "patience" and believing in your self that you can and you'd be surprise if you made it up to here, than you can go farther , but only if you want to of course. So keep at it and go up to the end until your child becomes a teen, you'll then know how well you did. Be proud, look up to your self unless you admire someone stronger than within yourself. O.k., than get ready for the teen life, you'll need to be stronger and wiser for that part. Otherwise, if you don't have strength within yourself, you can't control your own child, because it's considered that your child grew stronger than you.

YOUR BUSINESS AS PARENT

You'll need to support your child to a degree until your child can do for itself. Such as, but that doesn't mean that just because you're their parent you need to tell your child everything your child wants to know when you're having a personal conversation with anyone, especially your spouse. That's none of your child's business! That would be one of the hardest parts to remind your child that you would like some privacy at times. Your child needs to realize that the world does not revolve around your child. You as parents do need adult privacy. If you've taught this to your child ever since your child begin to understand. Than you shouldn't have any problems with your child giving you space. Don't let others especially families put you down just because you treat your child the way you do, if you know it's right, your child doesn't complain than it's just fine. Especially your parents, they need to go find a hobby instead of harassing you about how to raise your child. If anyone that cares and respects you, they wouldn't be telling you how to raise your child. Don't feel pitty for them that are whom will make you give up and do as they say. No one realizes that, but that's exactly what happens to everyone in the world. You as parents need to realize that you have a personal life to continue living aside with just your child and only your child. You'll lose that good relation with your child if you don't back-up and get some breathing space. And let your child realize that he/she needs time on his/her own too. So that your child can learn to think for himself/herself. Giving space to your child is when you can see if your child will make it alone out there in the real world.

CHAPTER 6
BEDTIME FOR YOUR CHILD

I don't know if you realize about your child that when it's bed time , that's when your child haves a lot to talk about and a lot of questions to ask, have you figured out "why" that's because your child just hates to go to bed. Bed time makes a child feel he/she is going to miss something. As parent you need to train your child that when it's bed time, that's it, it's time to go to sleep and rest. You don't need to stay in the room till your child goes to sleep, talk to your child about the day or read your child a story than kiss 'em tickle 'em, say "good night" get out, shut lights out your way out, remind your child you love 'em and that's it. If you don't play games, your child won't either. Of course every night make sure your child uses the bathroom, brushes its teeth and a bath before going to bed. "Don't" check on your child every 5 minutes just to see if your child went to sleep, just leave your child alone, sooner or later your child will go to sleep. If your child realizes you're checking on 'em that's going to keep your child up until you stop looking on 'em. Everyone automatically goes to sleep when they're sleepy, a child exactly the same way. Ignore your child's questions for the first couple of nights, if your child tries asking 'em for a while in bed. Just ignore it and before you know your child won't do it anymore. A child will do anything not to sleep. No question is important during your child's bedtime unless your child's sick or your home is burning. Those are the only reasons you should come into your child's bedroom and do listen to your child. As parent you train your child how you want your child to act and you stick with it the exact way you taught it to your child.

CHAPTER 7

WHEN THE SPOUSE
STAYS HOME

Did you know that when your spouse stays home to take care of the child, it's never been consider a job. That's very wrong!! A spouse whom stays home has a lot of responsibilities and work to do at home. It's just the same as going out to work in the city. Especially "man" don't think that when a woman stays home to care for the "child", its not consider a job, every out working spouse always think that caring for a child at home is too easy. Plus all they do is play, watch TV, take naps and eat. It's just that the out working spouse don't realize who's been keeping their child healthy, well mannered, disciplined and educated plus their home neat and cleaned. The working spouse never thinks of these things that are being done plus how hard it is for the home. The working spouse will never believe it nor thank the partner, for a great job he/she has doing everyday. As outside worker's job is from sun up till sun down, but an indoor worker with a child, their job is never done until the child moves out. Raising a child is a 24 hr job. It's worth it, but it's hard too. Nothing is easy in life unless you set it to be and you give it all you've got. The spouse whom stays home might not make nor bring any money home, but it sure does save a lot from not having to pay someone else to do indoor job plus pay someone else to raise the child. This is exactly what the out working spouse needs to realize and once in a while show appreciations to their spouse just the same way their boss appreciates them when they do a great job. Now by the outdoor spouse showing appreciation, to takes the place that's what gives the home spouse, energy, to continue going every day plus feeling better when the indoor spouse does anything. At times the indoor spouse will do something special for the out working spouse when appreciating is shown some way, not just by saying "Thanks" but by doing in bringing something small and nice, especially something the indoor spouse loves to receive at times, that's the best way you as the out working spouse will be doing it correctly. Now for those spouses whom stay home, watch T.V don't care for the child, talk all day on the phone, shop, get their hair done, and eat junk food E.T.C ….. No those aren't considering working at home. Those are consider "lazy bumps" by being the outside worker, you would love to come home and find a clean home, meal on the table and a behaved child, you know you need to always show appreciation to the home spouse, that's one way you'll get it, plus willing to pitch in at times when needed soon you get home. The out workers just don't realize how much work an indoor worker spouse has until they switch places for a few weeks. This is considering a full time job plus over time all year long with no raise. Raise your head high, be proud and feel happy about raising your child and taking care of your home because their isn't anyone whom can do it better than you.

CHAPTER 8

EXPLAINING "HOW" TO YOUR CHILD

The simplest way to explain "how" to your child is exactly the same way I'm explaining in my book on how to discipline your child, using simple words that your child can understand and explain it the way it goes and just repeating it until you've realized your child understand everything the way you wanted your child to understand. Than you let your child try and do whatever it's in the order it should be plus just see that it's being done correct. The worst you can do is lose your temper on your child just because your child doesn't get it on the first round. Remember, it's only a child will get it anyways. Once your child gets it, believe me your child will never forget it. Once you've explain "how" in words now then let your child try it with the hands, don't get mad if your child looses temper or gets a tantrum, that's normal in life (don't you loses when you don't get it?) Sometimes it helps the child understand it better by being that way. It never helps by you doing it for your child. Your child is going to need to learn "how" sooner or later, so why not start teaching your child now. Once your child got the hang of it you'll see a change on your child on how proud your child feels for doing it all by himself/herself. Of course do show proudness as parents once your child does the job correctly. Don't give your child pitty, your child doesn't need that, your child needs your support. When you're explaining "how" to your child, always stick with the same rules in the order you've started. Don't use big words when explaining "how" to your child or there'll be difficulty for your child to understand you. You as parents need to remember you're speaking to a child and not an adult. Put yourself on your child's shoes and see how you would like it if someone was explaining something to you with big words you don't even know what it means. Never give up on your child, you're the only ones whom your child has that can tell your child no and "how" life comes and goes at times.

CHAPTER 9

WHEN YOUR CHILD GETS SICK

As parents you should know very well when your child is really sick or faking it. Just because your child wants you, cries, acts like a brat etc… doesn't mean your child is sick all of the time. As parents you need to stop believing everything your child tells you when it's got to do with being sick. Plus small complains from your child shouldn't be taken too serious. Just check your child depending on your child's complain, if you don't think anything's wrong, than just tell your child that he/she will be fine and to continue whatever your child was doing, you continue doing what you were doing. Your child doesn't always really need you; your child just wants your attention at times. I don't think it's Important for your child to get what your child wants when your child wants it. This is when you need to just ignore your child if you know your child is fine. By you giving your child what your child wants when your child orders it, that's like letting your child know all he/she needs to do to what he/she wants. Which is to be a pain to mom or dad. This is where you learn to be very patient in life while raising a child. Don't give-up let it be your child who gives up when he/she starts to want something right now!! Well, just continue what you're doing and wait till your child loses all the energy and if your child starts to cry let your child cry, it's not going to kill them. When your child than realizes that by ordering mom or dad is not working your child will than quit being a little brat. Especially when your child is sick. When your child is very sick, than put your child to bed, give your child what he/she needs to eat and drink. Get out of the room; don't come in your child's room every 5 minutes. Would you like to be checked every 5 minutes by your spouse if you were sick? It's the same with your child just leave your child alone, never show your child that for being sick you'll treat him/her better and give him/her anything he/she wants. Wrong time to do that. Just keep treating your child the same as if your child was fine. Don't be so lovie-duby, that way just makes your child not feel better sooner. It's telling your child that only when your child is sick your child can then have all the love attention and affection from mom and dad at anytime and anything at anytime while being sick. Than your child will rather be sick everyday, just to have it his way. What do you think, wouldn't you if it was that way for you every time you got sick?

CHAPTER 10
?'S TO PARENTS FROM THEIR CHILD

In a child's age, the child doesn't realize what the child is asking nor does the child knows the difference between the question being asked and to whom should it be asked knowing it would be ok. Well, as parent you need to train your child in an early age that he/she is free to ask you any questions your child is not sure of the answer, and especially if your child doesn't understand the subject it's about. While your child is growing you need to give your child a chance to feel free to be able to talk with you. On any questions your child asks no matter what it's related to, you as the parent should always give your child will understand. Don't ever play around the bush when you're answering your child's questions, give it to your child straight. Unless you want to lose your child's respect about asking you about any questions. It's better if the answer comes from you, that way you'll know that in their mind it's in order. Parents should never ignore their child when their child haves questions. When parents start ignoring their child, they're losing their relationships plus that's when a child just goes to a stranger to find the answer and that's what you don't want to happen. It's very hard to get back a relationship with your own child. Funny it's easier to talk with a stranger's child than your own. But you think about it, which one is more important to you? If at times you can't answer your child's questions, you let your child know that. Never see your child's questions as if they we're funny nor cute. That's a parents biggest mistake for doing that and parents actually never notice what their doing until their child relationship start going down! Every question shouldn't be considered important but you'll need to explain it to your child why it's not important. Of course you're not going to be answering questions all day for your child. You make your schedule of when questions could be asked to you from your child. If you ignore the child, the child will start hanging around the bad crowed. Why should you wait till the worst happens to your child before you start giving your child attention? Don't because it's harder to try and get your child to normality. Your child gets more curious everyday, so grow with your child don't close 'em up nor ignore he/her. By giving your child the right answer and checking to see your child understand. Your child won't need chances and you're the only one who can give it so that your child won't needed it than, because it's very hard to get chances. . Now to those whom deserves that "chance" should get it. Especially your child. Teach your child how to earn the right   to get that chance he/she needs, deserves or earned. You'll need to explain it how you see it, it'll be easier coming from your mind. Explain it as easy as you can. And that'll make it a better way for both you and your child.

CHAPTER 11

KEEPING COMMUNICATIONS WITH YOUR CHILD

Just you imagine if us the people didn't kept in communication, how this world would really be? That's right miserable, well then look at it the same way with your child, especially because your child is just beginning to learn the facts of life. If your child is so important to you or even means a lot to you than prove it, that's by always keeping in communication with your child, no matter what it is. The more contact you keep with your child, a better relationship between you two will grow everyday. As parents that's the most important part of raising a child is keeping in contact. Not just once in a while, "EVERY DAY & EVERY MINUTE YOU CAN". Schools have to do more counseling to students and it's got to do that the parents have no communication with their child. That's not fair to the schools. By not staying in communication with your child, your child loses a lot in life. It slows your child down, doesn't get that self esteem a normal child should have for sure it's not a happy child. But you couldn't know any of this unless you keep in contact with your child, that way you'll always know what's going on in your child's life and how your child is doing in school or anywhere else. Your child will do so much better in your child's education. That's very important. By you as the parents keeping in communications with your child, it really helps & teaches your child to be the best your child can be in your child's life, you might not believe this but do it and watch what happens to your child in within time. All it takes is maybe a couple of words from you as parents just to turn your child around to be the best. It's got to be kept an open communication for there of everyday for your child's life no matter what happens, you got to stay in communication with your child. Believe me this will be something you'll be proud of after realizing that for keeping in contact with your child, you've made your child a better person plus you grew with your child, that's a very happy feeling. What do you think? To me it's proudness nothing else.

EYE CONTACT WITH YOUR CHILD

Teaching your child to look at you every time you're talking to your child or even when you call your child's name too is very important. Eye contact is one of the first ways you have, to communicate with your child ever since your child is born. You'd teach your child to look at you on your eyes when you are talking to your child, that way you'll know for sure your child is paying attention to what you're saying to your child. I believe a child can understand better when the child keeps eye contact with whom is speaking to him/her. Parents need to teach their child about looking at 'em in their eyes when they're speaking to their child. Life is the same way adult needs to look at the person whom they're speaking in the eyes when they're talking to each other or they just won't understand clear what they were supposed to. You know when you're in a crowd and you call your child, your child will automatically hear you and look for you, since your child is so used to looking at you when your child hears you calling his/her name. After a while you'll start making signs with your eyes in a way your child will know what it means whether if it was something good or bad that they just did or your eye signals would be telling your child if they're in trouble with you or not. Only you and your child would know what you're to get through to your child at that moment. Only a parent and they're child can understand the readings of your eyes. Kind of like your own language. Cool isn't it?

CHAPTER 12
PATIENTS

My believe that if you would only find that time as good as you found it to make those children. Than you should as well find it to educate and discipline those children. You shouldn't build what you can use. The most important thing to an adult becoming a parent is able to see their children grow and be brought up the best way they can. If you need to, look through so that you can teach your children the best knowledge you can. Maybe you'll even teach your self something you never knew. Most of everything that you really need for yourself before you start disciplining your children is "patients" otherwise it just won't work the exact way you want it to. Both you and your spouse have to be on this together. It'll make it alot easier if you both can make it that way. And if it's just one parent with whom the children live, you can still do it too. Either way you can really make it work and give the children very healthy educated life. Neither of you will regret these moments with your children. Do your best with your children everyday, because these days do not return and we have to always remember that no matter what, life moves on and not back.

If you take your children out then make sure you take the children to a place worth both your while so that you can both learn something out of the place, not just where there's pinball machines, bowling, etc.

Too much to learn about life and ourselves in places like that. Yes! Once in a while it's nice to go out and have fun in those places, but not always.

CHAPTER 13
EDUCATING YOUR CHILD

Usually students are considering "as" to the teachers every year when they first start school. Now, it's up to the student to maintain that grade till school is over for the year. As parent you need to consider your child with a very clear clean mind wanting and willing to learn as much as your child can from you whom your child sees and considers as the best teacher he/she will ever have and from whom your child is going to learn everything your child will be needing while growing up plus more. As parent while teaching your child all you'll be needing is "patience". In every subject you're going to want to teach your child with "patience" you won't make it through the last day without your child. Even before you start about educating your child, be sure you know you have the patience and as much as you're going to be needing while educating your child. (Sorry but you can't use that same kind of patience like in your favorite shopping mall). You should start teaching your child the minute you know your child can hear or see you. You'll need to repeat something a lot until you know your child has understood you. A child shouldn't be considering too small or too young to learn something. Anything is possible. First things you want to train your child would be to learn to talk, use the hands, smile, eat, take baths, brush teeth, crawl, walk, run, roll around, swim, get dresses and I'm sure you've got more. Now when your child started to get older that's when it's time to educate your child the correct subjects your child will be needing in life while growing everyday like, how to hold a pencil, write, read, work with numbers, easy way to spell, color, draw, read maps, put words to make sense, speak, health, music, exercise plus other extra subjects you know that will help your child while growing up. You should only teach your child a little of every subject you know, don't stick with one subject everyday after day, don't bore your child before your child gets interested in the subject. Now for the subject that are considered important to you but you know nothing of, well you should study on it then teach it to your child after you've comprehended it. Otherwise ask someone you know and trust very much to teach it to your child that way your child won't be behind when starting school and plus will know more and plenty while in school. When parents at home make and takes the time to teach their child about life, parents might not realize, but it helps a lot to teach their child to be a little ahead of certain subjects in school and even while growing up. Like I said if you're not a very patient adult to teach your own child what you should, then start practicing in having the patience because without being patient you won't be able to make it very far with your child and I'm sure this isn't what you'd want. One thing you need to train your child first would be for your child to be a very good listener for when you're talking and to always look into your eyes when you're talking to your child so that way your child is really listening to you. If you want your child to be strong in every subject and be able to face anything in life than you as a parent need to train your child that same way which is hard with love and care. There'll always be a child whom will just need to learn life the hard way and sometimes you as parents can't do much when the child is that way. The best you can do is train your child the best you know how and just let your child move on even if it's just going to be that your child will learn certain things in life the hard way. Don't worry those usually survive, just trust your child and give it time. As long as you've done your best than you shouldn't have nothing to worry about, your child will thank you someday, just don't expect it too soon. Hard headed kids usually take a little longer to comprehend things but at the end they always get it. Remember as parents you program your child's mind till the age of 5, usually whatever was programmed in your child's mind by the age of 5, that's what's usually that it's going to stay there, this is why you want to be careful on what you program on your child while young still before the age of 5. Just never give-up on educating your child as much as you want just be patient and you'll make it through before knowing you did. Of course a parent is never done in educating their child. Grow along with your child, walk the same path and enjoy life together with your child, this'll be moments you both will never forget nor would want to forget. It'll be worth every minute of your time plus more if you can spare it. Be proud of whatever your child selects to be in life. This was their choice, you as parent taught your child how to have and use the strength when needed. It's their life that they're going to have, be happy and proud of what you've made your child today.

TEACHING HOW TO CLEAN

We know a child likes to mess-up any areas in the house but hates to clean up after himself/herself, well that's too bad a child should be taught how to keep their playing area picked-up and the home cleaned. Nothings wrong with your child learning how to clean, just explain it very clear about how to use any cleansers and whatever else you use for cleaning. Do explain what shouldn't be done with these cleansers and what can happen if the cleansers are used on the wrong things. Don't just explain it to your child, let your child do the work while you're explaining, children learn faster by doing a job and not just sitting and listening to an adult talk. Once your child has learned, don't always say ~~to your child that the job was done great and that it looks~~ good when the job is still messy. Don't give credit unless earned the right way. If you don't teach your child about when something is done right and when something is done wrong, than who will? Don't have pitty, have your child re-do it. Does your boss ever have pitty for you? NO! There's no different here. Your child's room should always be kept neat. And picked up, stay on top of your child until your child has the hang of it and before you know it, it'll always be kept neat. Teach your child values to live by, once your child has values to live by, your child will be happy and proud.

CHAPTER 14

GIVING YOUR CHILD
A CHANCE

As much as you can teach your children you will probably learn yourself new things you've never expected to see. Every year there's always something new or a new way of doing things no matter what subject it is. When you're building something and your children are around you, have them help you. Let them do the parts about holding any machines that's needed, of course they will need your help if it's too heavy. Show proudness if they're able to do it, at least if they tried. Children's needs are their parent's proudness. That's what keeps them going and wanting to do other things more and more. Parents are like batteries to children that never shuts off, as much as children that never shuts off, as much as children are the same thing to parents because parents like to want to do more every time they see their children getting better at things they've been taught how to do and they are able to without it talking so long and doing it right, that's the best feeling a parent can feel, and the best a child can give to the parents.

CHAPTER 15

TRAINING YOUR CHILD HOW TO USE THE TOILET

Of course when your child is born your child still doesn't have control on its value moments. That's why you need to use diapers on your child till you believe your child is ready to be trained on how to use the toilet, at times when your child needs to go pea or release the value. Here's an easy way to train your child how to use the toilet:

Step 1= your child needs to know where the liquid is coming from and what it is.

Step 2= your child needs to know where is the value being released from and what's coming out of it

Step 3= now you just sit there with him/her to keep them company; before you both know it, he/she peed.

Step 4= for a boy have him go into the bathroom with dad to pee and just do everything dad does.

Step 5= for both when in needed to go to the bathroom, just sit them on the toilet, get them some fruits and little of their favorite food. Explain what the food turns into after eating it and what it turns to after eating it and through where it comes out from and why. By the time you've finished explaining, this child will have done some caca in the training toilet. Last exploration to your child will be that if that doesn't come out you can blow-up by keeping so much caca in their little butt. Of course, most of all at the end you'll be teaching them both how to clean their little behind after finishing and to the girl how she needs to clean her vigina too when being all done

Step 6= teach your child to flush the toilet every time your child does pipi or caca in it. But only if your child puts anything in the toilet is when they should flush it other wise don't touch it

Step 7= last but not least your child needs to know how to wash their hands every time they use the toilet, especially with soap too. Always congratulate your child if your child has used the toilet and did do something in it correctly. Give your child a little price, by just giving your child a hug and a kiss won't cost you that much. Your child appreciates that more than anything else. Give it a week doing the training like that and before you know, your child has learned to use the toilet all by themselves. Isn't that great or even fantastic!! Now if you don't want your child to do in bed, don't give him/her anything to drink 2 hours before going to bed. During the day see that your child uses the toilet every hour or ½ hour. No matter what you've given your child to drink or eat. It's just the point so your child will get use to knowing when to use the toilet and when not to.

CHAPTER 16
PUNISHMENT

Yes parents need to punish the child when the child's done something he/she wasn't suppose to nor caused allowed to but did it anyways, or when the child do so as told by parents nor doesn't follow rules the way it should be followed. A child should always be punished for not doing as told by parents. Punishment for children should be spanking their bottoms, smacking their hand when touching what it's not suppose to (enough that the child feels it), take away what the child plays with the most of the day, don't let the child watch t.v, take the child's electronics games, no use of phone plus no calls allowed, no desert, not allow to eat what the child enjoys the most, no company allowed, can't visit anyone, child not allowed to do anything fun, now, these punishments are the most that any child can get, believe me they work. Out of all these you select how many and for how long you're going to give it to your child. No questions about it, just that "if you wouldn't have done what you did, you wouldn't be in this position, now thinking about it". As parent you shouldn't feel bad nor let it hurt you more for punishing your child. That's considering that as parents you're feeling pitty and you don't really want to do it. That would be very strong to do that way. If you as parents never punish your child then your child will never learn what you want your child to learn "responsibilities". When your child gets older life gets harder. That's why it's better that the parents teach their child the correct responsibilities and the penalties they'll be getting if they don't follow the laws. If you have a lot of children, don't punish every child for one wrong thing one of them did, that's not fair. Only give the punishment to the one child who deserved it for what that certain child did. A child's age doesn't and shouldn't explain to the child exactly why he/she is getting certain punishments. Never let any child get away with what did or else you'll just be hurting the child and you're thinking you're just helping the child out. You'll always need to explain to your child what is the punishment, why and for how long.

CHAPTER 17

APPRECIATION SHOWN TO YOUR CHILD

Parents need to know how to show appreciation to their child before appreciating something. You as parent couldn't show appreciation to your child as you do to an adult. As parent, when you're ready to show appreciation to your child don't go over board with it. That's when a child gets mixed –up on how the child is really being appreciated or is just this luby duby from the parents. You as parents don't want your child to be like a brat, than don't realize that their doing it, you should pay more attention to the way you treat your child. Your child shouldn't be appreciated on every little thing they do, only when its something your child did and deep inside you feel proud and mostly surprised because of what your child did and how your child did it. If it was done wrong or incorrect, there shouldn't be any appreciation given, even though your child tried. In the real world no one will appreciate anything nor has thank-you for the bad job you did, even though you tried. Well why not start teaching your child the correct way, never put pitty just tell

JULIA BULLARD

your child to try again until it's done correctly. Your child
will learn better if you will admit the truth to -em and just
have your child do it over. So what if your child gets in a
"hissy mood", that won't cut it in real life. So just ignore
it and move on. As parents you need to grow with your
child while appreciating things your child does. As parents
when you're going to appreciate what your child did, the
best reward you can give your child would be a big hug, a
kiss on its cheeks and a short good prep talk related to what
your child did. That should only be done when your child
did a great job plus you realized how good your child did.
That's enough. If you show appreciation to your child for
every little thing your child does than you're teaching your
child the wrong ways of what appreciation really means. If
you'll notice that while your child is growing, you can still
show your child the same way you've always shown your
child appreciations. When it comes from a parent's heart
and mind, it doesn't cost anything to thank their child for
what its done. You learn to train your child and your child
learns to accept an appreciation the way you give it to your
child. If giving presents, items, stuff, and things e.t.c….to
your child is the way you show appreciations for what your
child has done, that's a very wrong way to do it. What are
you going to do when you don't have any money to buy
your child something because you've appreciated what your
child has done? Guess what happens? Your child will not be
doing anymore things for you, because you've trained your
child that only do something when you get something good
from mom and dad, a simple hug and a kiss will take you
far with your child wanting to do more just so that he/she
can be appreciated by mom and dad with a kiss and a hug.
You don't believe this, but you as parents are your child's
energizers', your child doesn't know either. Look at your
child when you give 'em a hug, kiss and thank them, you'll

find the sparkle and energy you've given your child for just a hug and a kiss. Now isn't that cheaper and don't you feel more happy for what you've just given your child? Yeap! A hug and a kiss from parents are the best memories for a child's life plus it's something no one can take away, they can always hold it in their heart for as long as they want.

CHAPTER18

NOT DOING WHAT YOU DON'T WANT YOUR CHILD TO DO:

Parents don't realize that their child is doing everything they are, until they see it with their own eyes and ask their child "who taught you this, where did you learned this, whom did you see doing this?" well, surprise! Your child got it from you. You don't realize, but as parents, you are your child's role model and guidance. As parents of course you were the first 2 faces whom your child will be seeing most of his life while growing up, so of course your child considers you his protector always. I believe a child's mind sees it, that if you're going to protect me I better respect you. Of course you and your spouse will always need to remember that if your planning to do something you both enjoy but it's wrong for your child to see you doing it at whatever age your child's in, then, you can't do it, because you'll have to answer questions to your child starting with "why" it's ok. Mom and dad can do this but the child can't. That's not fair to your child, so you need to remember what you don't want your child to do. (Than you can't do it either). Things like smoking, drinking, drugs E.T.C I'm sure you know the rest. It's not fair to punish your child for doing something wrong if these bad habits came from you and your spouse. I don't think that's fair, do you? No! So be more careful on what you plan to do when your child is with you at home.

CHAPTER 19
FINISH WHAT YOU START

Starting with the parents, they need to get use to completing everything they start, so that it'll train their child to become fully aware that it's really important to finish what you start before getting into anything else. If you don't show that you care about what your child is doing, your child won't complete the projects. Your child always needs courage and strength from the parents. You'll need to remind your child, why it's important to complete projects you start. If you never complete a project it'll never be able to really function the correct way like you as the child, you are a complete project, as parents you need to explain to your child that whether we like it or not we have to complete what we start. If your child learns at an early age that it's not important to finish what the child's starts a project, your child will always see life that way too. Every time your child can move on to another project, you make sure your child completes it, than in your child there are some things missing to complete your child's life and that is your child needs to always complete everything to be a "COMPLETE HAPPY CHILD" that way your child wont be leaving "life's important decisions" halfway undecided just because ever since he/she was small he/she didn't have to complete what he/she started. The parents never showed the child "how" nor explain 'why" you might not believe this but there's a lot that just stays with us while being raised and this is one of them. Tell me, is there something missing in your life? Sure, it's what you never completed in the past, I know you don't believe this, but it's hunting you down this means that you need to really think of anything you left behind way back in your past in completed (childhood, teen, at this age e.t.c) it's going to keep hunting you until you go back and just complete it or do what's needed to see that it's complete.. Your life will then feel different and of course fulfill and a lot better plus probably happier, just depends on the subject of course.

CHAPTER 20

INSTRUCTING YOUR CHILD WHAT IS THE RIGHT FOOD TO EAT

Well, if we go by what the world advices us to eat and what not to eat, we wouldn't be what we are today nor we wouldn't be where we're at either. As parent you should know what's the right and wrong food for your own child. Don't listen to others, just do it yourself. Your child should be able to taste different foods by you knowing it's good for your child. Number one food you shouldn't feed your child in "junk food". I'm sure you know what "junk food" is, things like, candy sweets, sodas, chocolate, cakes e.t.c…. what you don't give your child, your child doesn't eat. Of course you'll need to explain to your child why "junk food" is the only food your child shouldn't eat, plus it'll save you a lot of dentist bills in the future. Your only detail bill you should be getting is the once a year check-up. Parents have different ways of explaining the "junk food" problems, one easy way would be to find really nasty pictures and videos of kid's and people's teeth and directly telling your child that your child's teeth will become just like those teeth if he/she decides to eat "junk food"(incase your child thought of eating "junk food" behind your back) do remind your child that no matter whose he with, your child should not eat "junk food", it'll still be bad for your child's teeth. So what if your child thinks those pictures your showing are grouse or maybe your child throws-up because of what you put your child to see, that means it's working, just you think for yourself, you would try it or eat it after you've seen what "junk food" can do to you? I know I wouldn't but that's only my opinion, incase you want to eat something sweet but you don't want your child to eat it just because you are than, as parent you're going to need to eat your sweets at times when you're child is not with you nor watching you for every move you do. Other wise you're going to need to explain to your child "why" you are eating sweets after knowing what sweets do to your teeth. Of course you should teach your child how to take care of his/her teeth the proper way. Your child should know that your child's teeth should be brushed after every meal "why" because that's what helps your child have very good and healthy teeth. A clean teeth expression: anything your child dirties will need to be cleaned "right?" well, that's exactly the same thing your child should realized that your child is doing with its teeth or otherwise your child's teeth will then get like those pictures you showed your child which I don't think your child liked. Plus you'll be saving a bundle in the years not to have to take your child to a dentist unless it's for the check-up. When you want your child to understand you clearly, than speak clearly in your adult way. Do ask for questions about the subject you just spoke.

CHAPTER 21

OUR CHANCES WHILE TIME FLIES:

From our childhood to our adulthood we all change in certain ways whether we want to or not. Of course with a good mind a person changes to a better life, if the mind doesn't function right, you'll turn into an unnormal person. The most important thing to remember is that when you are going to begin a family you're going to need to know for your self how to discipline & educate a child if you don't know by now than it's time to explore books and ask questions about every subject in disciplining & educating a child. So that when your child is born you'll be ready and even more proud of yourself because you've learned so much on how to educate & discipline your new child. Yes do listen to families & friends when they went to show you a certain way of how to do certain things with your child, but "no" you don't have to do it with your child if you don't feel too sure about it. As long as you listen to those people they'll be fine, that way it doesn't turn into an argument and you'll have nothing to worry about. Yes there'll always be someone who'll say that they been on this child raising for a little longer than you. So! That doesn't always mean they know what's better for your child. No one knows what's better for your child but you the parents. Unless you have questions because you're not too sure about certain things to do to your child and you just don't feel too safe about it, than that's when you call someone you feel knows a little more about what you're about to do to your child. Only call the ones you feel comfortable talking to and won't fill you up with too much bull for just one little question. Our parents did their best in raising us. Well now we use our parent's knowledge, plus more to raise our child. As parents the best part is you get to raise your child the way you want to not the way the world says, one part our parents sometimes can't let go is that our lives ourselves changes, we're grown adult and we now know what's right& wrong in life. So now it's time for you to share with your child the best you can in raising your child, that's where the parents at home come in their child's life and show their child how to be strong everyday they can. Don't expect that "thanks" from your child for raising your child very strong, you'll get it, just be patient and you'll be hearing it in a way your child has never thanked you before in life.

CHAPTER 22
YOUR CHILD'S FRIENDS

A friend to your child is like your child having a second part of your child's self. You should be able to tell when your child has a very good friend, your own child will tell you about the new friend your child has and how much your child and the friend enjoy each other's company, how much   fun they always have, if they can't be apart that they have to even call each other on the phone and talk for hours about a lot of personal things about themselves. Now, that's what does consider a friend. As parents, you'll need to talk to your child about how to select a very good friend. The best way will be that not everybody you see or talk to is considered a good friend to your child. A very good friend is another someone whom your child gets along very well,   works together, never argues without a good reason, enjoys   each other's companies and does a lot of good reason, enjoy eachothere's companies and does a lot of goods and fun things together, friends come and go, but a true friend would never leave your child. They'd always find someone to keep in touch even if they're living miles apart. Every friend your child finds is not a good friend. There'll be friend your child brings home and of course as parents you'll never approve of them, but if you learn to talk with your child without arguing about your child's friend than your child will see your point of view of why you don't like your child's friends at times. Your child will think about it and in time your child will than let go of that certain friend, if that friend doesn't seem to be worth keeping. Just don't make it a big issue or you'll just make it harder for your child to get rid of that friend, by screaming, yelling or even insulting your child's friend that won't help a bit. As parents, just calm down and go cool before saying anything to your child you're going to regret later in life. As parents you need to remember that no matter what happens, life still goes on. This part of life your child will need to learn sometimes the hard way which is by not wanting to believe nor listen to by himself/herself even mom nor dad. Don't worry your child will survive, he/she has before "RIGHT!" but do remember your child's life will go on no matter what.

CHAPTER 23
STREET CHILD

If you hope & wish that your child doesn't turn into a street child like those out there you've seen suffering, starving. Using drugs, using alcohol having sex at an early age just to survive, stealing, dying, and getting diseases plus other more bad things your child's to become. Than you as the parent need to learn and remember the biggest lesson that's given for this reason. Which is to always keep an eye on your child, stay in communication with your child, know what your child is watching on TV, stay in contact with your child's teachers, make sure your child has done the homework's, check it, have a parent child conversation (fit it into your schedule) if all this isn't done everyday than that's when your child feels neglected and goes out into that world and does very bad things that shouldn't be done, goes to jail steels, do a crime and your child then becomes what you never thought your child would turn into. As parents you don't realize that when your child was born the big "responsibility" as parents you were going to have. Well it's time to know as much as you can, so that you can give the best way you can to your child while raising your child. You'll learn how to raise your child like everyone does, which is day by day. You'll never realize the mistakes you're making to your child until you see it yourself and correct it right there, so that it won't happen again. But you as parent raising your child, it's like teaching and learning something you never thought you were ever going to learn. It's the best experience you'll ever see happen in your life plus you'll never regret it, as parent you'll always treasure those times you've spent with your child. After your child has grown into a mature adult which had made something great out of your child's self than that's where you as parent will realized how well you did your job while raising your child. Then it's when you can then give yourself credit for what you've been doing and for how well your job was done. As a parent you should never give-up on your child especially if your child turns into a street child. This is when your child really badly needs you, don't never turn your back on your child, and remember as parent you should always be there for your child, no matter how bad the situations are. Your child can always correct its own mistakes as long as you as the parents will be there to help your child get up and show your child that you'll be right by the side no matter how bad it'll be and for as long as your child will be needing you. Don't never turn your back on your child, you're the only ones your child will have and the only ones your child can count on. Prove this to your child, this will be the first to open your child's needs will really want to do better and see itself to the right direction in life. Give your child the best you can as a parent, that's all you can do. The best a parent to give their child is love, trust and to let their child know they still believe in their child to do the right choices in their life. This is how as parent you'll pick energy to your child. You as parent don't believe this will never change. Your child will always call you first when your child gets in trouble or can't make-up its own mind or certain decisions in your child's life. You'll always be your child's top priority in your child's life forever.

CHAPTER 24

YOUR CHILD, GOING TO THE MOVIES

Before answering "yes" to your child's question "can I go to the movies?" as parents you should know what movies your child is going to see and what's it's rates plus most of all what it's going to be about. If you don't know much about the movie your child wants to see, than you should find out. Ask someone you trust that has seen the certain movie to tell you about it, and than you decide. Movies now a days aren't really any good for children to watch, no matter what it's rated. Whether it's scary., spooky, dirty, funny & grouse movies are the worst movies for your child to watch because your child doesn't realize until your child's mind begins to wonder the wrong directions than starts to dream about things your child never seen in your child's life, so of course it's going to scare your child to heck, you might even have to take your child to see a psychiatrist, to see what's needed to be done, so that your child can return back to acting being normal before your child had started to see that certain movie. Just because as parent you weren't interested in what the movie your child was going to watch now, what it was going to be about, you can come out paying thousands & thousands of dollars for the rest of your child's life and not have a normal happy child before beginning to watch that certain movie just because as parent you didn't want to sit with your child and watch the movie together. Yes, just one movie can destroy a child's way of being and acting.

CHAPTER 25

BEFORE GOING TO A RECREATIONAL CENTER

The first step you'll need to do before taking your child to a recreational center is to sit your child down, make sure your child is looking at you when you're talking to your child. Give your child the rules of regulations to where you're going plus remind your child what you'll be expecting from your child while being in this place. The best rules to give a child are to always stick with you no matter where you're at; don't interrupt when people are talking, listen to what the person is trying to say, don't be a little brat, don't wine, listen to me when I'm talking to you, don't ask to buy anything, most important of all, if you lose your child or if your child loses you, you're going to need to explain to your child not to panic nor cry because it doesn't help. Your child won't find you any faster by acting that way. Remind your child to find a security guard, policeman, or any of the people whom works in that certain place where you're at, tell your child to have any of them help your child look for you. Make sure your child carries important phone #"s and you should teach your child how to call collect incase your child doesn't have any money. If when you give all these rules to your child and your child has any questions about it, answer them now because it'll be too late later. Other wise you're all ready to go and have a great time. Good luck!

CHAPTER 26
SPENDING NIGHTS

No, it's not one bit important nor necessary for your child to spend the night at friend's house. Well, you as   parent need to explain "why" your child can't spend nights at a friend's homes. When your child and the friend goes to bed, it's time to shut their eyes and go to sleep, it's not time to play, talk, clown around, play games nor watch TV e.t.c than in that case just keep your own child in his/her own bed. Tomorrow they can continue where they stopped. Now slumber parties I consider an expectation because on slumber parties I consider an expectation because on slumber parties they stay-up very later and have fun plus parents can't complain because it's a very special day for their child and they allowed their child to have a slumber party after knowing everything they had planned to do for that night. When friends spend nights, parents would not like it to be like a slumber party all the time. Than don't let your child's friend spend nights, of course if an emergency happens in the family, that's understanding for a child to spend couple of nights at a friend's home with the parent's permission. Two very close friends are together all day long what else do they expect after the day is over to continue by spending nights at each other's home? "Wrong" just explain to your child that the sooner your child goes to bed the sooner tomorrow will come and your child and the best friend can continue having fun. But the longer your child argues with you, the longer it will be before tomorrow comes. That's all you need to say. It should be the same explanation to your child's friend whom would like to spend the night at your house too. If your child sleeps at a friend's home too many times it's very bad because than your child will begin to pick-up bad habits you're not going to like and you'll realize that very soon. That'll be the last thing you would like your child to do.

CHAPTER 27
FEAR OF THE DARK

The dark is something to learn at an early age, not to be afraid of it. That starts with the parents teaching it. I started my child at a very early age, when my child was 5-6 months old I kept all the lights off in the night in my child's bedroom. For every night my child went to bed. So by doing it that way every night, it taught my child that being in the dark is O.K and he was never afraid. My child after a while that he realized no one was around nor any lights were on, meant to close his eyes and go to sleep till the next day light didn't meant anything to be afraid off. I try to make stories out of the noises my child heard. Lighting I told him those were people bowling up their in the sky and I smile with it too, when the house squeaked I reminded my child that it's just the house setting to go to sleep like him because it's dark, animal noises I told my child that it was the parents calling their children it's their bedtime just like I do to him when, it's his bedtime too. I don't talk to my child about bad and spooky things, what my child doesn't know won't hurt nor scare him. There's no reason to explain to child long stories about spooky stuff if it's not important. The dark is just a part of our day. Our lives are a part of the day and the night. Nights are beautiful because of many reasons. We can see things that we cannot see during the daylight hours. The child starts very early to look at the parent and see if the parent is afraid, if the parent is laughing, and it sends a signal to the child. "everything is o.k., and fear goes away I started very early with my ideas and not giving lights on in the child room was the beginning of realizing that going to bed at night meant going to sleep with no fears.

FEAR OF NOISES

When out house squeaked and made noises, I told my child that the house was going to sleep just as he was settling down, if animal noises from outside bothered my child I merely told him the parents were calling their kids to go to bed before night

CHAPTER 28

WHEN & WHAT SHOULD A CHILD WATCH ON T.V

If you let your child just watch anything he/she wants on TV than you're taking a chance and not caring about what your child watches and if you do than you'll begin to see how easy your child will pick-up any habits and become something you wished he/she didn't. A child is very bright in their own way when they want to do & learn something, they know how to do the bad things first, (want to or not, child or adult will always wish they didn't, that's just part of life) and T.V is the number 1 place where they'll always pick –it from, real fast & learn it really easy with no problems, this is why you want them to think about or learn about TV is consider a baby-sitter. Your child can pick a habit very easy since you're not paying much attention to it. It'll just get worst or cause trouble to your child, until becomes a big deal than is when you'll starts caring, "wrong" sometimes it's too late then, to try to solve it, but you should give it a try on solving it since you love your child. Explain to your child why you think what he/she is doing is not so good, especially because it gets them in trouble. This is the same way it can cause a child trouble by reading and your not knowing what the child is reading about. It is very important that both parents always stay on top of their child to know and be up to date with what's going on in the child's life day by day and not just check with them once in a while. Parents don't realize that making a child is not as easy as it is to raise them. Raising a child is like raising a speed you've planted and you would hope it grows-up bright & healthy with no problems ahead. Well unless you water that seed and keep it healthy until it can go on its own, it's the same way any child, of course a child needs more attention at times. So as parent you need to be able to direct them on the correct path as they grow. Don't expect it today but someday that child of yours will "thank you" for being who you were and always being there for the child when he/she needed you. That will be your time to feel proud of yourself and be happy for what you've achieved. That work you'll always see it on anything your child does or achieves too. Remember, want to or not you have to put all the time you can in your child so that your child can learn the different between wrong & right, saying anything once to a child's mind, you're going to need to repeat it for a while at different time until you can really realize that it's really hammered in that mind of the child. You'll realize it on your child when it's really already hammered in. You'll even feel more proud of your self plus you'll want to even do more and get better at it while teaching anything to your child. Always explain it as it is to your child without "playing around the bush" or you'll mix the poor mind. Don't you like an explanation to be clearly explain to you without making-up any un-needed words? Always stay in touch with your child, day by day not just when you have bad news or good news to tell your child, that's not fair to your child. Your child needs to know always what's going-on now, later and in the future. Your child would feel better and be much happier in his/her little life for now, at least your child won't be worried, when a child worries too much, that slows the child in thinking and doing better for the day. I don't think you'd want that to happen to someone you love very much. You'd be miserable too. Nothings wrong with explaining very clear about a problem to your child, your child might be small on the outside but their mind can take a lot, just give it a try and be very patient while talking to your child, you'll be surprised on what your child understands. Talking to a child is like you looking up a word on the dictionary and just reading its meaning till it makes sense to you right? Get to your child's level when you're explaining something you want your child to really understand you and you'll be surprised at your own self on how much your child understood. Of course it takes a lot of time but at least you know that every second counts and every minute was worth it for your child whom you love very much and you want your child to always know as much and you want your child to always know as much as your child can know as long as it's good and it's part of living a great life everyday. All it takes is "patience, time and a lot of love" to start with and it will never end, instead love grows bigger & bigger everyday. You'll never realize this unless you sit to think about it and know the big different between your child's life ever since your child was born and how much your child has accomplished today, when that occurs you need to remember that if it wasn't for you, your child wouldn't had gone this far in life. By listening to your child just the way you want to be listening to when you speak to someone, you'll realize how much it's just better to explain something in a very simple way to your child instead of baby talking to your child every time you need to explain something, no matter what it is. Explain it straight out as it is and never give-up until you know yourself that your child understood everything the way you wanted him/her to. The best way to know that your child did understood you in everything you explained are to ask the child if he/she understood everything you said and if so than have your child explained it back to you. For sure if your child can repeat back to you about what you just said to him/her than you would have nothing to worry about because you know your child understood you and if not than try to explain it a little slower and with easier words in your sentences that would be easier for your child to understand. Once you have your child repeat what you just said to him/her they'll learn to listen more carefully to you in the future because they're going to realize that they're going to have to repeat it to you, kind-of like a daily test everyday it keeps their mind opened & sharp for the next explanation or conversation you're about to tell them. You won't need to have your child repeat everything for the rest of their life, just till you realized you're self that your child is now paying more attention and is listening to what you're talking about plus doing as he's/she's told than you cans top asking your child to repeat it to you. It becomes a habit afterwards you can than yourself just stop asking your child to repeat it to you because you know yourself that your child is really listening and doing as he's/she's told to. It's like when something is being explained to you and you than get it, so it doesn't have to be explain again and again to you, doesn't that make you feel great when you get it on the first time? You'll realize that your child will even be happier once he/she starts getting it on the first go around because that way it'll give you time to love your child more & more every second of the day. The more you can really show your child that you love 'em, that's kind of like energizing your child for a better life everyday. Your child will always see you as their top priority who kind-of knows a little more of life than they do until they themselves realize that they can catch-up to your level and even pass by talking the right direction to life. As parents we need to give our child the courage, strength, braveness, pride, knowledge & the best life we can to really be able to show them what is considered a great life and so that they themselves can live it & be happy too. You always remember, nothing is hard to teach a child, you love, ask yourself how did you learned and was it worth learning it, yes! Well, then I believe it's time to share what you know with someone you love the most in your life, so that they can learn how to make happiness in their life and be successful on anything they do.

CHAPTER 29

LENDING MONEY TO YOUR CHILD

As parents you should lend money to your child just the way banks lend it to their customers. "But" before lending money to your child, you'll need to explain with clear detailed information to your child about borrowing money from you. Just like when you as the adult borrows from the bank. You'll need to make a very clear short child's agreement between the two of you how much the child's borrowing, with punishments that will happen to the child if the loan is not paid as set, on certain days of the week. With dates until last payment on certain date. If not you'll need to explain as example what the child's punishment will be every time the child misses payments, punishments are: no friends allowed to visit, you can't visit your friend, no electronic games can be played, no T.V, you can make a list of x-tra chores too, you can add other punishments too, otherwise this all needs to be done until payment is due. Oh don't forget about explaining the best part, the percentage you'll be getting because your child borrowed your money. These punishments are just when you punish your child when your child did something wrong, your child has survived them; I believe your child will survive these few punishments if any rules are broken. I see nothing wrong with that. If as parents you don't teach your child to learn the value of money the accurate way than who will? By your child paying you on time always, it trains your child to be on time on all things in life. Remind your child that not anything out there is really "FREE" your child needs to be reminded that anything your child wants; your child will have to work for it, because as parents you shouldn't give them everything they ask for. If you want the best for your child, teach your child the best of your knowledge in money and if you don't feel you don't know enough then read and learn about it just before your child gets to the borrowing age, that'll be your choice.

CHAPTER 30
TEACHING HOW TO COOK

Number one step about teaching your child how to cook is to tell your child the kitchen rules you expect to be followed. Don't play with the fire; don't touch anything on stove without a pad, the kitchen isn't a playhouse, listen carefully, ask questions e.t.c….plus your own rules you feel your child needs to remember. Your child needs to know how to use the measuring, whether it's by spoons, cups or any other ways. Your child needs to know how to control what your child turns on. Your child needs to know how to use a timer, read instructions on the food your child is about to cook. Have your child work in the kitchen by himself/herself once you know your child can do it. Teach your child what to do incase of a fire, show your child where the first aid kit is. Explain in the clearest way you can to your child and make sure your child understands you, have your child ask questions about anything in the kitchen and cooking, work with your child while explaining, do the cooking together. It'll be more fun to your child if you'd work more with your child speeches about cooking. Last rule about cooking would be to wash everything you dirty plus always clean your areas. Remind your child that when you come into a clean kitchen, you leave it even better than what you've founded in. Otherwise your child will not be allowed to work in the kitchen again. The earliest food to teach your child when beginning would be, canned food, salad and some boxed food too. Don't exaggerate yourself if your child gets burned, just take care of the burn and move on.

The End